FUN FACT FILE: SPORTS!

20 FUN FACTS ABOUT BASEBALL

By Ryan Nagelhout

Gareth Stevens
PUBLISHING

Please visit our website, www.garethstevens.com. For a free color catalog of all our high-quality books, call toll free 1-800-542-2595 or fax 1-877-542-2596.

Library of Congress Cataloging-in-Publication Data

Nagelhout, Ryan.
 20 fun facts about baseball / Ryan Nagelhout.
    pages cm. — (Fun fact file: sports!)
 Includes index.
ISBN 978-1-4824-3965-6 (pbk.)
ISBN 978-1-4824-3966-3 (6 pack)
ISBN 978-1-4824-3967-0 (library binding)
1. Baseball—Miscellanea—Juvenile literature. I. Title. II. Title: Twenty fun facts about baseball.
 GV867.5.N26 2016
 796.357—dc23

                                             2015025574

First Edition

Published in 2016 by
Gareth Stevens Publishing
111 East 14th Street, Suite 349
New York, NY 10003

Copyright © 2016 Gareth Stevens Publishing

Designer: Sarah Liddell
Editor: Ryan Nagelhout

Photo credits: Cover, p. 1 Eugene Onischenko/Shutterstock.com; p. 5 Jim McIsaac/Staff/Getty Images Sport/ Getty Images; p. 6 Moondyne/Wikimedia Commons; p. 7 Slowking4/Wikimedia Commons; pp. 8, 26 Transcendental Graphics/Contributor/Getty Images Sport/Getty Images; p. 9 Nate Shron/Stringer/ Getty Images Sport/Getty Images; p. 10 Dennis Ku/Shutterstock.com; p. 11 Christian Petersen/Staff/ Getty Images Sport/Getty Images; p. 12 JASON TENCH/Shutterstock.com; p. 13 (background) David Lee/ Shutterstock.com; p. 13 (Kauffman Stadium) Jamie Squire/Staff/Getty Images Sport/Getty Images; pp. 13 (Dodger Stadium), 15 Ffooter/Shutterstock.com; p. 13 (Marlins Park) Mike Ehrmann/Staff/Getty Images Sport/ Getty Images; p. 13 (Fenway Park) Rich Gagnon/Stringer/Getty Images Sport/Getty Images; p. 13 (Wrigley Field) Steve Broer/Shutterstock.com; p. 13 (Yankee Stadium) Pierre E. Debbas/Shutterstock.com; p. 14 Jam Media/CON/Contributor/LatinContent Editorial/Getty Images; pp. 16, 24 Mark Cunningham/Contributor/ Getty Images Sport/Getty Images; p. 17 Delaywaves/Wikimedia Commons; pp. 18, 23 Eric Broder Van Dyke/ Shutterstock.com; p. 19 Getty Images/Staff/Getty Images Sport/Getty Images; p. 20 Jason Miller/Stringer/ Getty Images Sport /Getty Images; p. 21 Jonathan Daniel/Stringer/Getty Images Sport/Getty Images; p. 22 Diamond Images/Contributor/Diamond Images/Getty Images; p. 25 Andy Lyons/Staff/Getty Images Sport/Getty Images; p. 27 Underwood Archives/Contributor/Archive Photos/Getty Images; p. 29 Boston Globe/Contributor/Getty Images.

Printed in the United States of America

CPSIA compliance information: Batch #CW16GS: For further information contact Gareth Stevens, New York, New York at 1-800-542-2595.

Contents

Baseball's Home 4

Double Nay 6

Major League Baseball 8

In the Park 12

Playing the Numbers 14

Fantastic Feats 16

Big Plays 20

Hang On! 22

Weird Baseball 24

Women on the Diamond 26

Extra Innings 28

Glossary 30

For More Information 31

Index 32

Words in the glossary appear in **bold** type the first time they are used in the text.

Baseball's Home

Cooperstown is a tiny town of about 2,000 people on the shores of Otsego Lake in central New York State. So why is this little town home to the National Baseball Hall of Fame? The ballpark next door is called Doubleday Field. It was named after Abner Doubleday, who was said to have invented baseball in Cooperstown.

It's a great story, but is it actually true? Let's step into the batter's box and take a swing at baseball's most famous facts.

Was baseball really first played in Cooperstown? Read on to find out!

Double Nay

FACT 1

Only one man said Abner Doubleday invented baseball.

A former pitcher named Al Spalding owned a sporting goods company. He claimed Doubleday invented the game, the diamond shape of the field, and the word "baseball," in 1839 in Cooperstown. No **proof** has ever been found. In fact, Doubleday wasn't even in Cooperstown in 1839!

Doubleday never mentioned baseball in his own writing, and articles written about the military man never mentioned the game until after Spalding's claim.

Abner Doubleday

On March 15, 2011, Major League Baseball (MLB) **commissioner** Bud Selig put together a Baseball Origins Committee, which was a group to find out where the sport came from.

FACT 2

No one knows where baseball came from!

Baseball grew out of many different sports. Many people believe two early English sports, cricket and rounders, were the basis for baseball. Early games similar to modern baseball were called stoolball, poison ball, and goat ball!

FACT 3

Major League Baseball is actually two different leagues.

The National League (NL) was founded in 1876. The American League (AL) was a **rival** league that signed a National Agreement in 1903. This agreement said both were "major" leagues and the winners of the two leagues would play in a World Series to crown a **champion**.

The first World Series was played between the Boston Americans and Pittsburgh Pirates in 1903.

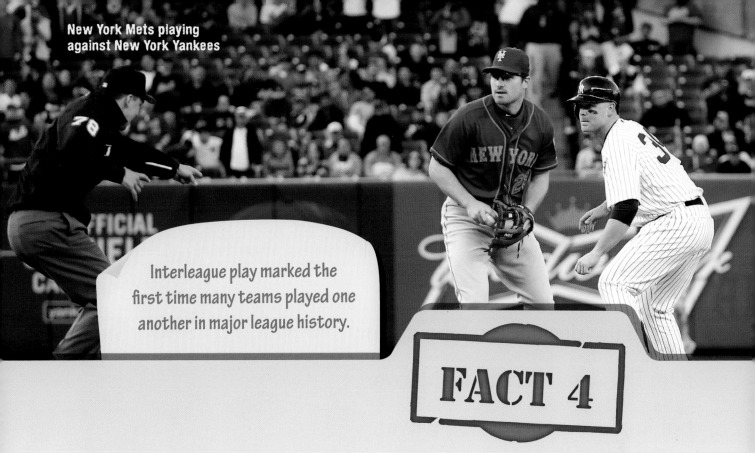

New York Mets playing against New York Yankees

Interleague play marked the first time many teams played one another in major league history.

FACT 4

Until 1997, AL and NL teams only played against each other in the World Series.

The 1997 season marked the first time MLB had interleague play, or play between teams in the two leagues during the regular season. Before that, American and National League teams only played teams in their own league.

FACT 5

American League pitchers usually don't have to bat.

On January 11, 1973, the AL added the designated hitter (DH) rule. The rule lets a certain player bat in place of a position player, usually the pitcher. The DH, however, doesn't play in the field. Many people think the National League should adopt the DH rule, too.

Boston's David Ortiz has the most career home runs as a designated hitter.

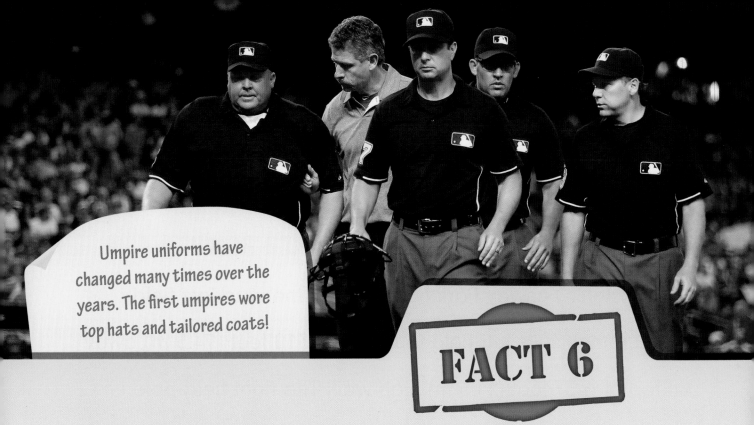

Umpire uniforms have changed many times over the years. The first umpires wore top hats and tailored coats!

The AL and NL used different umpires until 2000!

When teams played interleague or World Series games, the umpires would be from the home team's league. AL and NL umpires even had different uniforms! The umpire unions **merged** in 2000, and all game officials worked both American and National League games.

FACT 7

No two major league parks are alike!

Boston's Fenway Park has some of the wackiest field measurements! Its left field foul pole is 310 feet (94.5 m) away on top of a 37-foot (11.3 m) high wall! The right field pole is just 302 feet (92 m) from home plate.

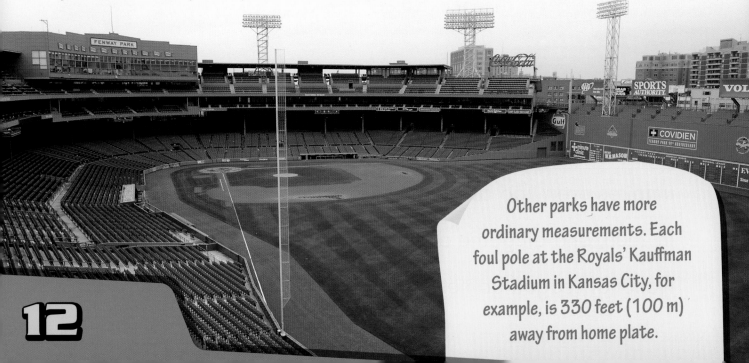

Other parks have more ordinary measurements. Each foul pole at the Royals' Kauffman Stadium in Kansas City, for example, is 330 feet (100 m) away from home plate.

Fence Facts

LEFT FIELD 330 FT **CENTER FIELD** 410 FT **RIGHT FIELD** 330 FT

KAUFFMAN STADIUM
KANSAS CITY, MISSOURI

LEFT FIELD 330 FT **CENTER FIELD** 395 FT **RIGHT FIELD** 330 FT

DODGER STADIUM
LOS ANGELES, CALIFORNIA

LEFT FIELD 355 FT **CENTER FIELD** 400 FT **RIGHT FIELD** 353 FT

WRIGLEY FIELD
CHICAGO, ILLINOIS

LEFT FIELD 314 FT **CENTER FIELD** 418 FT **RIGHT FIELD** 335 FT

YANKEE STADIUM
NEW YORK CITY, NEW YORK

LEFT FIELD 310 FT **CENTER FIELD** 390 FT **RIGHT FIELD** 302 FT

FENWAY PARK
BOSTON, MASSACHUSETTS

LEFT FIELD 314 FT **CENTER FIELD** 418 FT **RIGHT FIELD** 335 FT

MARLINS PARK
MIAMI, FLORIDA

Playing the Numbers

FACT 8

Major league batters try to stay above the "Mendoza Line."

Batting below the Mendoza Line is an average below .200, which is less than one hit every five at bats. It was named after Mario Mendoza, a shortstop with a career .215 average who struggled at the plate.

Although Mendoza's career batting average was actually above the "Mendoza Line," the name quickly became a clubhouse joke and stuck.

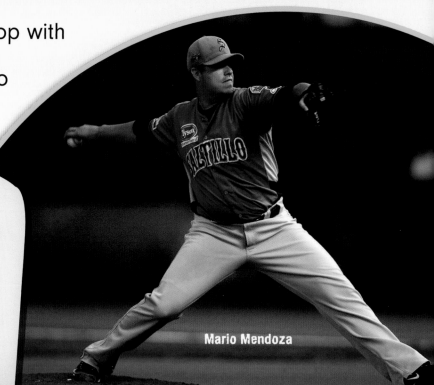

Mario Mendoza

Baseball Stats

Statistics help us understand baseball better all the time.
Here are a few stats you should know!

BA	OBP	ERA	E
BATTING AVERAGE The number of hits a player has divided by his number of at bats.	**ON BASE PERCENTAGE** The number of times a batter reaches base divided by his plate appearances.	**EARNED RUN AVERAGE** The number of earned runs a pitcher allows divided by how many innings he pitched, multiplied by nine.	**ERROR** A mistake made by a player in the field.
R **RUN** A point given to a team when a player reaches home safely.	**RBI** **RUNS BATTED IN** The number of runners brought home by a player when at the plate.	**H** **HIT** A ball put in play that lets a batter reach base safely.	**SO (K)** **STRIKEOUT** When a pitcher throws three strikes or a batter swings and misses three times.

FACT 9

The National League's Triple Crown hasn't been won since 1937!

Triple Crown winners in baseball are players who lead their league in batting average, home runs, and RBIs. In 2012, Detroit's Miguel Cabrera won the AL Triple Crown. It was the first time since 1967, when Boston's Carl Yastrzemski won the crown.

Pitchers also have a Triple Crown that's won more often, in which a player leads the league in wins and strikeouts and has the lowest ERA.

Miguel Cabrera

One of the best hitters ever left baseball twice to serve in the armed forces!

"The Splendid Splinter" missed three seasons serving as a pilot in the Navy during World War II from 1942 to 1945. He also missed games in 1952 and 1953 serving with the Marines in the Korean War.

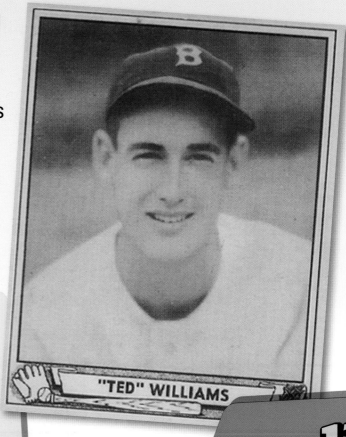

"TED" WILLIAMS

In 1941, Williams hit .406 and led the league in home runs, walks, runs, slugging percentage, and OBP. He's the last player to hit over .400 the entire season.

FACT 11

"The Wizard" broke an 84-year-old record for most hits in a season.

On October 1, 2004, Seattle's Ichiro Suzuki broke George Sisler's record for most hits in a season (257). Suzuki finished with 262 hits on the year, 101 more hits than he played games that year! He also had 242 hits in 2001, his rookie—or first—season!

Ichiro led the American League in hits seven times in his career.

Ryan pitched for the New York Mets, California Angels, Houston Astros, and Texas Rangers during his 27-year career.

FACT 12

Nolan Ryan has the most strikeouts—and walks—of all time.

Ryan has more "Ks"—5,714—than innings pitched—5,386—and leads all other pitchers by more than 800 strikeouts. His 2,795 walks and seven career no-hitters—complete games without allowing a hit—are also major league records!

FACT 13

An unassisted triple play is one of the rarest plays in baseball.

The unassisted triple play is when a player gets all three outs in an inning without help from other fielders. It's happened just 15 times in the history of Major League Baseball. In 1920, Cleveland second baseman Bill Wambsganss made the play in the World Series!

Only infielders have ever completed the unassisted triple play in the majors. Cleveland second baseman Asdrubal Cabrera completed one in 2008.

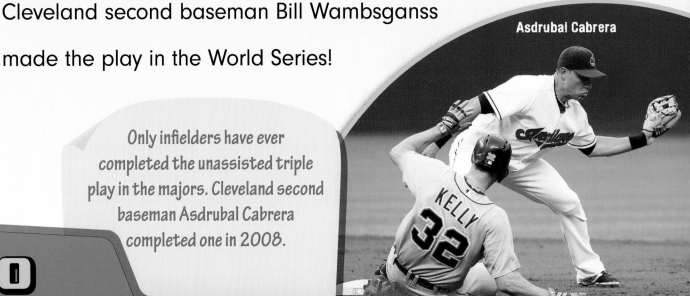

Asdrubal Cabrera

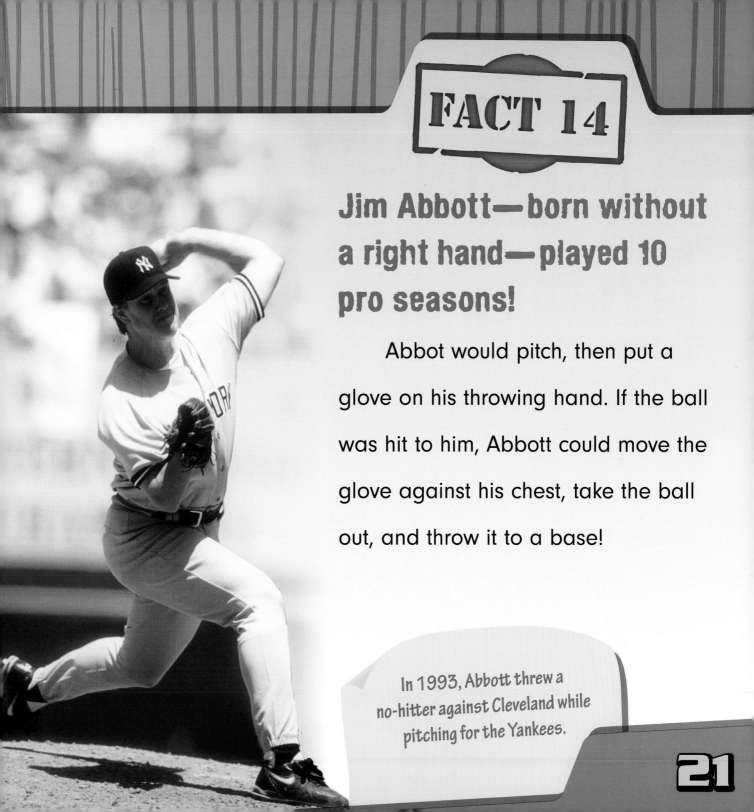

Jim Abbott—born without a right hand—played 10 pro seasons!

Abbot would pitch, then put a glove on his throwing hand. If the ball was hit to him, Abbott could move the glove against his chest, take the ball out, and throw it to a base!

In 1993, Abbott threw a no-hitter against Cleveland while pitching for the Yankees.

Hang On!

FACT 15

George Brett

Batters can use pine tar to get a better grip—but not too much!

Only the first 18 inches (46 cm) of a bat handle can be covered with the sticky stuff. In 1983, Kansas City slugger George Brett was called out after hitting a home run against the Yankees with a bat umpires said had too much pine tar on it!

The Royals **appealed** the umpire's call, and the game's last four outs had to be replayed a month later. The Royals won, 5-4.

Teams also use a special detergent to get out stains from pine tar.

FACT 16

Teams clean their uniforms with a special baseball detergent.

When baseball uniforms get dirty, many teams use a detergent called Slide Out to clean uniform tops and pants. It's designed to remove **stains** from the red clay used in many infields. It also gets out white line paint and grass stains!

FACT 17

Every baseball is rubbed with mud before it's used.

The mud, called Lena Blackburne Baseball Rubbing Mud, has been used for decades in the majors. The mud, from a **tributary** of the Delaware River, takes the "sheen" off new baseballs and lets players grip them more easily.

In 1938, Lena Blackburne was a third base coach for the Philadelphia Athletics when he started using mud to treat baseballs.

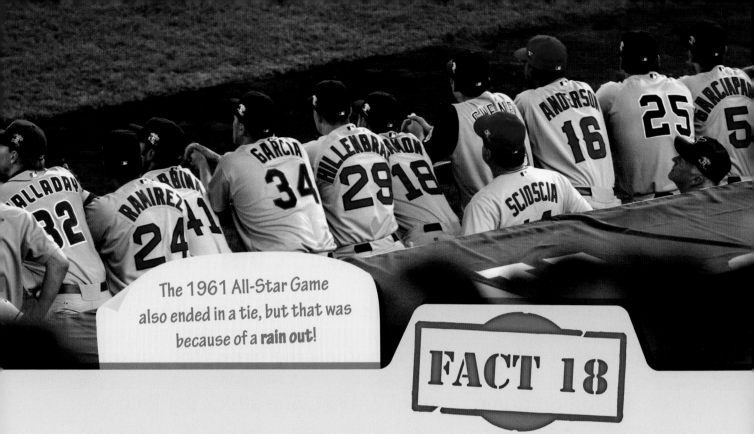

The 1961 All-Star Game also ended in a tie, but that was because of a **rain out!**

The AL and NL All-Star Teams once ran out of pitchers!

The 2002 MLB All-Star Game ended in a 7-7 tie after 11 innings. Both managers played all 19 of their pitchers to get everyone playing time. MLB commissioner Bud Selig had to call the game a tie, and fans booed both teams off the field!

Women on the Diamond

FACT 19

A 17-year-old girl once struck out Babe Ruth!

Jackie Mitchell, sinkerball pitcher for the Class AA

Chattanooga Lookouts, pitched against the New York Yankees

in an **exhibition** game on April 2, 1931. She struck out Ruth on

a called strike, then fellow Yankee great Lou Gehrig swung and

missed at three

straight pitches!

Lou Gehrig

Babe Ruth

Jackie Mitchell

To this day, people debate whether Ruth and Gehrig were really trying to get a hit against Mitchell, but she claims they were!

Lots of women have played baseball by "barnstorming," or playing on teams that travel the country without joining a league.

FACT 20

Lizzie Murphy was the first person to play on both leagues' "All-Star" Teams.

"The Queen of Baseball" played a few innings at first base with the American League All-Stars in 1922 in a game against the Boston Red Sox. In 1928, she played in an All-Star Game with the National League All-Stars.

Extra Innings

Baseball is a quirky game full of weird and wonderful facts. Major League Baseball alone has more than a century of history filled with oddities. Did you know the longest baseball game in Major League history went 25 innings? They had to stop the game and finish it another day!

Then there's this wild fact: Reds catching great Johnny Bench could hold seven baseballs in his bare hand. The stats, records, and amazing players are part of what makes baseball so fun to watch—and play!

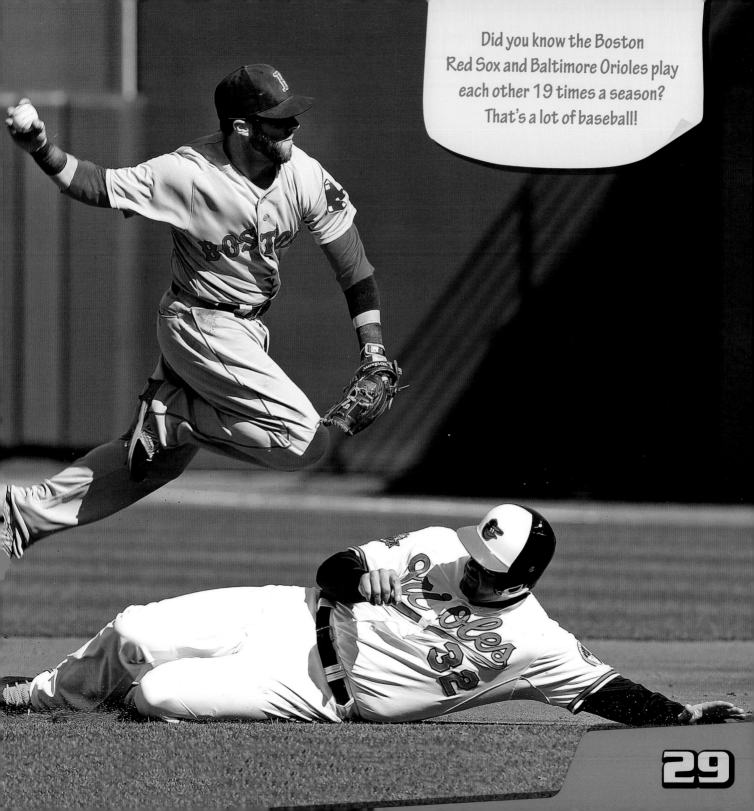

Did you know the Boston Red Sox and Baltimore Orioles play each other 19 times a season? That's a lot of baseball!

29

appeal: bringing a case to a higher authority

champion: the overall winner

commissioner: an official in charge of a group

detergent: matter used in cleaning

exhibition: a public showing that doesn't count in the record books

merge: to come together

percentage: part of a larger whole given in parts out of 100

pine tar: sticky matter made from pinewood

proof: facts that show truth

rain out: the stopping of a game due to rain

rival: one of two people or groups that compete against each other

stain: spot or soil

tributary: a stream or river flowing into a larger body of water

For More Information

Books

Clay, Kathryn. *Cool Baseball Facts*. Mankato, MN: Capstone Press, 2011.

McCully, Emily Arnold. *Queen of the Diamond: The Lizzie Murphy Story*. New York, NY: Farrar, Straus and Giroux, 2015.

Pina, Andrew. *Baseball's Greatest Records*. New York, NY: PowerKids Press, 2015.

Websites

Baseball Reference
baseball-reference.com
Find more stats about your favorite team and players at this great site.

Major League Baseball
mlb.com
The official site of Major League Baseball has information about all 30 pro teams in the United States and Canada.

National Baseball Hall of Fame
baseballhall.org
Find out more about the history of America's pastime at the Hall of Fame's official website.

Index

Abbott, Jim 21

AL 8, 9, 10, 11, 25

batting average 15, 16

Cabrera, Asdrubal 20

Cabrera, Miguel 16

Cooperstown 4, 5, 6

cricket 7

DH 10

Doubleday, Abner 4, 6

ERA 15, 16

Fenway Park 12, 13

field measurements 12, 13

hits 15, 18

Ichiro Suzuki 18

interleague play 9

Kauffman Stadium 12, 13

Lena Blackburne Baseball Rubbing
    Mud 24

Mendoza, Mario 14

Mendoza Line 14

Mitchell, Jackie 26

Murphy, Lizzie 27

National Baseball Hall of Fame 4

NL 8, 9, 10, 11, 25

OBP 15, 17

Ortiz, David 10

pine tar 22, 23

RBI 15, 16

rounders 7

Ryan, Nolan 19

Slide Out 23

SO (K) 15, 16, 19

Spalding, Al 6

stats 15

Triple Crown 16

umpires 11, 22

unassisted triple play 20

Williams, Ted 17

World Series 8, 9, 20